Wrestling

Chris St John

First published in 2015 by Wayland

Copyright © Wayland 2015

Wayland, an imprint of
Hachette Children's Group
Part of Hodder & Stoughton
Carmelite House
50 Victoria Embankment
London EC4Y 0DZ

Series editor: Rasha Elsaeed
Editor: Julia Adams

Produced by Tall Tree Ltd
Editor, Tall Tree: Neil Kelly
Designer: Ed Simkins

Dewey number: 796.8'12-dc22

ISBN: 978 07502 9704 2

10 9 8 7 6 5 4 3 2 1

Printed in China

An Hachette UK company
www.hachette.co.uk
www.hachettechildrens.co.uk

Picture credits
All photographs taken by Michael Wicks, except;
t-top, b-bottom, l-left, r-right, c-centre
4 Dreamstime.com/Pniesen, 5 Li Gang/xh/Xinhua Press/
Corbis, 8 Getty Images, 17tr Dreamstime.com/Galina
Mikhalishina, 19 Dreamstime.com/Galina Mikhalishina,
23tl Kristin Fitzsimmons, 24 Dreamstime.com/Peter
Muzslay, 27tl Marcello Farina, 29 Tim Hipps

The website addresses (URLs) included in this book were
valid at the time of going to press. However, because of
the nature of the Internet, it is possible that some
addresses may have changed, or sites may have changed
or closed down since publication. While the author and
publisher regret any inconvenience this may cause the
readers, no responsibility for any such changes can be
accepted by either the author or the publisher.

Disclaimer
In preparation of this book, all due care has been
exercised with regard to the advice, activities and
techniques depicted. The publishers regret that they can
accept no liability for any loss or injury sustained. When
learning a new activity, it is important to get expert tuition
and to follow a manufacturer's instructions.

Acknowledgements
The publishers would like to thank the Slough
Wrestling Club.

Contents

What is wrestling?

Wrestling is an exciting, fast-paced competitive sport that combines strength with speed and agility. Of the many types of wrestling found around the world today, two styles – **Freestyle** and **Greco-Roman** – are competed at the **Olympic Games**.

An ancient sport

Wrestling is one of the oldest sports in the world and dates back thousands of years. Paintings on ancient Egyptian tombs built around 2000 BCE show competing wrestlers. In ancient Greece, from about 1100 BCE to 145 BCE, wrestling was the most popular sport. A points system was awarded for various moves, similar to the points awarded in modern wrestling today (see page 9).

Two wrestlers grapple during the Nadaam Games, a traditional sporting event in Mongolia where participants take part in wrestling, horse racing and archery.

Folk wrestling

There are hundreds of types of local, or folk, wrestling around the world. In the UK, styles include Catch-as-catch-can (also found in the US) and Scottish Backhold. Japan has Sumo, a form of wrestling that dates back many centuries. In Mongolia, traditional wrestling has been practised as a sport and martial (fighting) art for nearly 2,000 years.

Wrestlers will try to throw one another to the floor and pin each other's shoulders to the mat. Here, Xu Li of China in red throws Ana Pacal of Romania during in the 2008 Beijing Olympics.

Modern wrestling

The object of both Freestyle and Greco-Roman wrestling is to throw an opponent to the floor and **pin** their shoulders down on the mat. The main difference is that Greco-Roman wrestling bans any holds below the waist or any trips to throw an opponent to the mat. Other forms of wrestling that are particular to one part of the world are called **folk wrestling**. Wrestling is a sport that is open to both men and women, and taking part in wrestling encourages the development of strength and fitness.

Top tips

The best way to learn Freestyle or Greco-Roman wrestling is by joining a local wrestling club. Coaches at a club can teach you the correct wrestling techniques and provide advice on all aspects of wrestling training.

Equipment and mats

When you set foot inside the wrestling ring, you will want to wear an outfit that allows you to move freely, grip the mat and not give your opponent an advantage.

The singlet

A wrestler's outfit consists of a one-piece vest and shorts uniform called a singlet. The singlet is usually tight-fitting, as any loose clothing would give an opponent something to grab hold of and pull you to the mat. However, the singlet should not be so tight that it restricts movement during a competition.

Singlet

Knee pads

Singlets are usually made from a tight-fitting material that will hug a wrestler's body so that there is nothing for an opponent to grab hold. It should also stretch to allow for plenty of movement.

Wrestling shoes

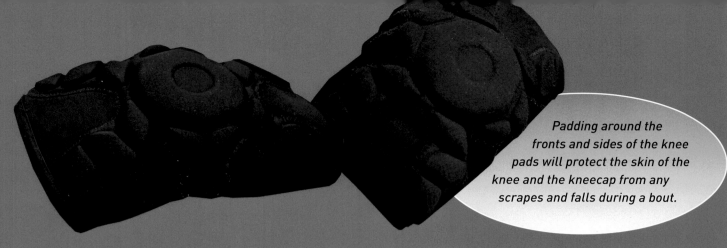

Shoes and protection

Wrestling shoes are usually trainers specially designed to support and protect the ankles during a **bout**. The soles of wrestling shoes should also provide some grip on the mat. Ears are squashed during close-quarter grappling, so it is a good idea to wear headgear. This consists of two padded shields worn over the ears and straps to hold them firmly in place. A pair of pads will protect your knees when the action moves to the floor.

Many modern wrestling shoes are fastened using velcro straps. These straps can be fastened and adjusted more quickly than traditional laces.

Wrestling arena

In top-level Freestyle and Greco-Roman wrestling, the competition area consists of a large circle measuring 9 metres (29.5 feet) across. The central wrestling area lies at the middle and measures 7 metres (23 feet) across. Around this is a 1-metre (3.3-feet) wide ring called the passivity zone. When wrestlers move into this area, the bout is stopped and restarted from the central circle, a 1-metre (3.3-feet) wide circle, which lies at the middle of the **arena**. Surrounding all of this is the protection area and wrestlers will be penalised if they step into this zone.

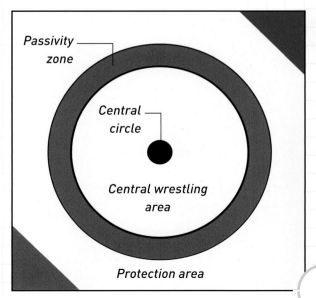

Passivity zone

Central circle

Central wrestling area

Protection area

The wrestling contest

The object of a wrestling competition, or bout, is the pin, or fall – to hold both of your opponent's shoulders to the mat for one or two seconds. Sometimes, a pin is not possible, so judges are on hand to award points for the completion of successful moves.

Judges

A wrestling contest is overseen by a team of three judges – the referee, the judge and the mat chairman. The referee oversees the bout inside the ring, while the judge sits to the side of the mat keeping score and helping the referee with some decisions. The mat chairman keeps time and rules on technical decisions during the bout. The judges decide on the success of certain moves and award points to the wrestlers.

A referee pays close attention as two wrestlers compete during the quarter-final of the Men's 60 kilogram Greco-Roman event at the 2008 Olympics.

Weight classes

Wrestlers are divided up into groups of similar weights, or classes, to compete against each other. There are seven classes. For men, these range from 55 kilograms (121 pounds) to 122 kilograms (269 pounds). For women, the range is 44 kilograms (97 pounds) to 72 kilograms (159 pounds).

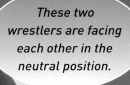

These two wrestlers are facing each other in the neutral position.

The leg clinch is used to restart the floor action in Freestyle wrestling.

The par terre position is used to restart the floor action in Greco-Roman wrestling.

Winning a bout

A bout is divided up into three two-minute periods. The winner is the wrestler to win two of the three periods. During each period, points are awarded to wrestlers for successful moves, such as a takedown or a reversal, or against them if they are penalised – for example, if they step out of bounds or strike an opponent. Alternatively, a wrestler can win the whole bout by successfully completing a pinning move. Each period starts with the wrestlers facing each other in the standing **neutral position** to wrestle on their feet. After about a minute, the wrestlers will stop and move to the floor, with the wrestlers starting off in either the leg clinch or the **par terre** position.

Points system

In Greco-Roman and Freestyle, wrestlers are awarded points for certain moves:
Takedowns – throwing an opponent down onto the mat from a standing position. One to five points awarded, depending on the success of the move.
Reversal – turning a defensive position into an attacking one.
One point awarded.
Exposure – exposing an opponent's back to the mat without achieving a pin. Two or three points awarded, depending on the success of the move.
Penalty – awarded against a wrestler for breaking the rules. One or two points to the opponent, depending on the severity.
Out-of-bounds – awarded against a wrestler for placing a foot in the protection area. One point awarded to the opponent.

Preparing the body

Wrestling is a sport that relies on strength, fitness and speed. Looking after your body by exercising and eating well will help you to compete at your best and avoid injuries.

Top tip

While you are performing physical warm-ups, prepare mentally by telling yourself how you will put your skills into practice in a wrestling bout. This will help you get your mind as well as your body ready for action.

Fitness and warming up

It is important to warm up before undertaking any form of hard exercise. A good warm-up should include some light jogging to get your heart beating faster and some stretches to prepare your muscles for the fast, energetic moves in a wrestling bout. Improving fitness allows you to compete for longer and may give you the edge over an opponent. Fitness, or stamina, can be improved with distance running.

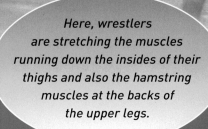

Here, wrestlers are stretching the muscles running down the insides of their thighs and also the hamstring muscles at the backs of the upper legs.

Strength exercises

Wrestling uses muscles all over the body, and any exercises to increase strength should reflect this. It is important to work on core strength (developing the body in the trunk), as well as the legs and upper body. Make sure you get the advice of a qualified coach before carrying out any exercises. Good exercises for wrestling include lifts and carries, press-ups, lunges, jumps and wall-sits.

Press-ups will improve your upper body strength to help with lifts and throws.

Wall-sits will improve your leg strength and stamina, allowing you to compete for longer.

Different lifts will help improve your technique and increase your leg strength.

Diet

Wrestlers should eat food that contains plenty of vitamins and minerals, especially fresh fruit and vegetables, to help them stay healthy. Foods that are high in protein will help with muscle strength and development. Wrestling uses a lot of energy, and wrestlers should also eat energy-rich foods, such as rice and pasta.

Posture and levels

There are several basic skills a wrestler needs to master in order to compete in the ring. These techniques can be put together to create the moves that will win a competition.

Posture

Wrestlers need to keep their bodies in the correct posture at the start of and during a move. If you do not have the correct **posture**, you could leave yourself open to an attack, or, worse still, injure yourself while performing a move.

Top tip

When moving, start by stepping with the foot closest to the direction of movement – if you are moving to your right, take the first step with your right foot. This will prevent you from losing your balance.

This wrestler is standing with a good posture. His feet are wide apart and his head and body are above his legs.

When viewed from the front, you can see that the wrestler's posture and broad stance give him a solid base.

Here, the wrestler is leaning too far forwards. His weight is in front of his feet, which means he is unstable.

Movement

Wrestling is not a static sport – it involves a lot of movement as wrestlers grapple to achieve a superior position and throw an opponent. When moving, wrestlers must remember to maintain a good posture so that they do not lose their balance and expose themselves to an attack.

This wrestler is moving forwards, taking a small step with his right foot.

With his right foot planted, he takes a second small step with his left.

This wrestler's stance is narrow and unstable.

He has corrected his stance by stepping outwards.

Changing level

Successful attacks usually involve approaching an opponent at different levels, either high around the shoulders, in the middle around the waist, or low around the legs (unless taking part in Greco-Roman wrestling, where holds below the waist are banned). It is important that you maintain good posture while approaching at these different levels.

The wrestler in red feints an attack to his opponent's shoulders.

He then drops and moves in low to attack his opponent's legs.

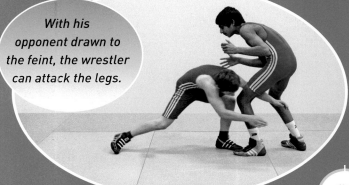

With his opponent drawn to the feint, the wrestler can attack the legs.

Penetration and lifting

In order to get opponents on the floor and achieve a takedown, you need to lift them off their feet. However, this can only be achieved once you have been able to get inside an opponent's defences using a **penetration** move.

Stepping inside

Penetration involves stepping inside an opponent's guard to attack the legs, hips or upper body. It can be tricky, as you have to move lower than usual and any loss of balance will give an opponent an easy opportunity to throw you to the floor. The two most common penetration moves to attack the legs are the outside-step and the centre-step.

The wrestler on the right has penetrated his opponent's defences using an outside-step move. He has stepped with his left foot outside his opponent's feet.

Centre-step

1

The wrestler on the right steps forwards, placing his right foot between his opponent's feet.

2

He then drops to one knee and keeps moving forwards to attack his opponent's legs.

In the air

Lifting is used in both Freestyle and Greco-Roman wrestling, although lifts below the waist are banned in Greco-Roman wrestling. Lifting opponents off their feet means that they are fully in your control – they cannot counter-attack without any support. As with penetration, posture is key to lifting. By keeping your back straight and using your legs, you will find lifting easier and are less likely to strain your back. Lifts can be achieved using one or both legs, and from in front of or from behind an opponent.

Throughout a lift, it is important to keep your head up and avoid bending your back. This will avoid hurting your back and neck.

The wrestler in red has stepped inside his opponent's defences and driven his shoulder into his opponent's waist.

He drops his hips and bends his knees, keeping his body over his legs.

By pushing up with his legs, he is able to lift his opponent clear from the floor for a spectacular takedown move.

Back-step and back arching

As well as lifting, you can unbalance opponents by using the **back-step** or by **back arching**. Both techniques involve lifting opponents off their feet, either by stepping in and twisting or by arching your back.

Top tip

Practise both the back-step and back arching by stepping through the moves without an opponent. This will help you to develop the correct feet positions and posture to perform the techniques.

The back-step

Using the correct footwork is key to the back-step. Performing the back-step involves twisting, so that you are facing away from your opponent. Doing so could expose you to a counter-attack, so it is vital that you maintain good posture. When carried out correctly, the throwing wrestler should complete the move on top of an opponent, pinning him to the mat.

Back-step throw

1 The wrestler on the right steps in, twisting his foot.

2 He twists his hips into his opponent.

3 Rolling forwards, he pulls his opponent over.

4 He ends the move by landing on top.

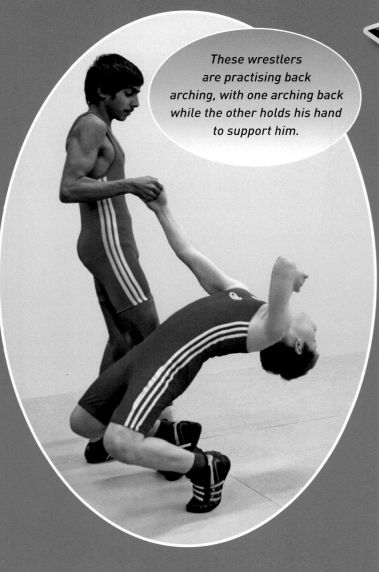

These wrestlers are practising back arching, with one arching back while the other holds his hand to support him.

Pommelling

To carry out a throw, wrestlers need to get inside an opponent's defences. During a bout, you will see two wrestlers knock and push each other using their arms and hands. They do this in order to break down each other's defence, so that they can get a good grip on their opponent's body. This grappling and grabbing is called **pommelling**.

Back arching

While back arching takes a great deal of practice to master, it can produce the most exciting throws in wrestling. As with the back-step, body posture is key to successful back arching, and it is important to push your hips under your opponent so that you can use your legs to lift. If you do not get your hips underneath, you could hurt your back. Back arching also uses level changes to get underneath an opponent's defences.

Skills drills

There are a number of specific **drills** that will help you to improve and perfect individual wrestling skills. All of them will allow you to work on your posture, so that you can maintain the strongest position throughout a bout.

Top tip

Good balance is essential. Your feet should be placed so that you always maintain your balance. Keep your elbows tucked in. Only take small steps, except when attacking your opponent.

Moving and grappling

Getting into the right posture and keeping it are vital to good wrestling technique. Even when carrying out simple movement drills, it is important to keep a good neutral posture, so that you know how to hold your body in a strong position. A simple levels drill will help you to develop the skills necessary to change the angle or area of attack against an opponent and gain a superior, controlling position.

Levels drill

The wrestler in red steps forwards with his left foot.

He steps through the other wrestler's legs, keeping his head up.

Star file

BUVAISAR SAITIEV
Olympic champion

Buvaisar Saitiev is one of the most successful wrestlers of all time. Competing in the 74 kilograms (163 pounds) and 76 kilograms (168 pounds) classes, the Russian athlete won six **World Championship** titles between 1995 and 2005 and three gold medals at the Olympics.

Rolling and lifting

On the floor, it is important to play to your strengths and use your body's strongest muscles. Rolling practice will teach you how to prevent injury by using your strong shoulder muscles instead of your weaker lower back. Similarly, learning how to lift will stop you relying too much on your back and will show you how to use your leg muscles correctly.

This wrestler is rolling around on his head, practising good movement technique for floor work.

Pommelling drill

The wrestler pushes his arm inside his opponent's.

As he does so, the wrestler twists his body to his right.

Once completed, the move is repeated with the left.

19

 # Takedowns and counters

Individual wrestling skills are combined to create more complicated techniques that can be used in a bout. The first two techniques to look at are takedowns and **counters**.

Takedowns

A takedown involves taking opponents off their feet and down to the mat. Takedowns use many separate skills, including penetration, lifting and back-step skills. Leg attacks can focus on one leg or two, and there can be many variations, including a simple back-trip, a post-and-drive, or even a fireman's lift. Upper-body attacks feature throws using the head, chest or arms.

Double leg attack

1. The wrestler in red drops to attack his opponent's legs.

2. With his arms around both legs, the wrestler drops his hips downwards.

3. He then twists and drives up, taking his opponent to the mat.

Arm throw

1. The wrestler in red steps in, pushing his right arm under his opponent's left.

2. As he rolls forwards, he pulls his opponent over his shoulder.

3. As his opponent hits the mat, he lands on top to try and pin the shoulders.

Counters

Even when being attacked by an opponent, it is important to stay alert for the opportunity to counter-attack. You might be able to take advantage of an opponent's mistake, or you can block an attack before launching your own. Counters involve combining blocks to different kinds of attack (either to your legs or your upper body) with attacking moves that suit the body positions of both yourself and your opponent.

Sprawl and crossface

1 The wrestler in red spots his opponent's attack and steps back.

2 He then drops, or sprawls, on top of his opponent.

3 The wrestler spins around to the 'crossface' position to attack from the side.

Here, the wrestler on the left has spotted an attack and performed a snapdown. He grasps the back of his opponent's head to pull him to the mat.

Escapes and reversals

When the grappling moves to the floor (see page 9), the wrestler who starts off in the bottom position of the par terre is at a disadvantage. This wrestler can score points by either escaping from this position to the neutral stance, or by reversing positions and ending up on top.

(see page 9)

Top tip

If you are in the bottom position, your first move to escape must be explosive. Force your opponent to react so that you can create an opening to escape or reverse the position with your next move.

Escaping

The key to a good **escape** is to be aggressive and quick. While trying to escape, it is important to maintain a good posture and to gain control over your opponent's hands to stop them from applying any moves. Make sure that your legs and hands are kept underneath your body, so that you are not unbalanced. You should also keep your back square-on to your opponent, so that they are not able to get around your side, from where they could push you over.

Escape to neutral

The bottom wrestler is about to escape.

He starts by attacking his opponent's grip.

With one hand free, he twists his body, while attacking the other hand.

With both hands free, he stands up into the neutral position

Star file

KURT ANGLE
Freestyle wrestler

US wrestler Kurt Angle won the World Championship title in 1995 in the 100 kilograms (220 pounds) class, and the gold medal in Freestyle at the 1996 Olympics. He now performs bouts for TNA (Total Nonstop Action Wrestling).

Reversal

A reversal involves turning the tables on an opponent to take control and achieve a pinning move. As with an escape, any movement needs to be fast and aggressive, in order to unbalance your opponent. Once unbalanced, you should aim to take your opponent to the mat to pin them and win the bout.

Reversal — floor

Here, the wrestler in blue is about to perform a reversal.

He steps round to one side, pulling his opponent forwards as he does so.

With his opponent unbalanced, he pulls out any supporting arms.

Reversal — standing

The wrestler in red pushes down to break his opponent's grip.

As he does so, he spins around to attack his opponent from behind.

Once behind his opponent, he can throw him to the mat using a back arch.

23

Breakdowns and pinning

A defending wrestler in the bottom position must try to escape or reverse the position. As he attempts to do so, the attacking wrestler in the top position will try to 'break down' an opponent's defences and go for the pinning move.

Breakdowns

When you are in the top position, you have the advantage because your hands are free to launch attacks. Being above an opponent also means that you can bring your weight down on them and tire them. Keep looking to break down any defences, so that you can unbalance your opponent. You could try faking a **breakdown** in one direction. Then, as your opponent counters the move, quickly attack them in another direction.

You can unbalance your opponent by tripping their feet, grabbing their hands or by twisting their body and pushing them down to the mat.

Outside ankle breakdown

1

2

The wrestler on top grabs hold of the outside ankle. This is the ankle farthest away from him.

He pulls the ankle back sharply, pushing the defending wrestler down onto the mat.

Pinning moves

Pinning is the ultimate objective for any wrestler – pin your opponent to the mat and you win the bout, no matter how many points have been scored. Once a breakdown has been achieved, it is important that you press home your advantage and flip opponents onto their back, so that both shoulders are held to the mat for a couple of seconds.

Half nelson pin

1

The wrestler in blue slides his left arm under his opponent's left arm.

2

He drives forwards, pulling up with his left arm to roll his opponent over.

3

He completes the move by pinning his opponent.

Cradle pin

1

2

3

The attacking wrestler wraps his arms around his opponent as shown.

He then drives forwards, rolling his opponent over onto his upper back.

With his opponent's shoulders on the mat, he completes the pin.

Technique drills

Working on specific areas of various wrestling techniques will help you to perfect your range of moves. Learning to combine techniques will enable you to fully exploit any wrestling situation.

Drills and spills

There are hundreds of different wrestling drills. A simple spin drill, for example, will help you to practise keeping your knees off the mat, while a roll reversal will hone your reversal skills while on the floor.

Spin drill

One wrestler crouches on all fours, while the other rests his chest on his back.

The top wrestler spins around, keeping his knees off the ground.

Roll reversal

The defending wrestler in red is below his opponent in the par terre position.

The defending wrestler rolls forwards, pulling his opponent with him.

The drill is finished with the defending wrestler pinning his opponent.

Star file

SAORI YOSHIDA
World champion

Saori Yoshida started competing at international level in 2002. The Japanese wrestler never lost an international bout from her debut until 2008, notching up 119 consecutive victories in the 55 kilograms (121 pounds) class. Between 2002 and 2014, she won twelve World Championship titles and Olympic gold medals at Athens in 2004, Beijing in 2008 and London in 2012.

Changing attack

It is important to stay alert to your opponent's moves and be prepared to change your own plans should the need arise. Sometimes, your opponent might successfully block an attack and you will need to react quickly, otherwise you could end up having to defend.

Single to double

Here, the wrestler on the left has stopped the attacker's single leg attack.

The attacker reacts quickly and moves his left hand to attack both legs.

Double to single

The wrestler on the right drops to attack both of his opponent's legs.

The defending wrestler has spotted this attack and stepped back with his left leg.

Reacting quickly, the attacking wrestler switches the move to attack one leg instead.

 # Taking it further

Wrestling is a technical sport that requires hours of practise and physical training. Finding yourself a local club will give you access to training facilities, as well as other wrestlers to fight against.

Top tip

Always try to stay calm and confident when competing with other wrestlers. Respect the decisions of the judges, and do not let the actions of your opponent – or their fans – affect your determination to win the bout.

A wrestling coach will be able to provide class teaching as well as one-on-one instruction.

Finding a club and coach

Local and national organisations will have the contact details of a club near to you. You can find this information by checking out the relevant websites on the Internet. Once you are part of a wrestling club, you will have access to competitions at all levels, should you wish to take your wrestling to the next level.

Wrestling competitions

Competitions are organised for wrestlers of all ages, abilities and sizes. These range from club-level competitions, through regional bouts, right up to national and international competitions. In the US, wrestlers at schools, colleges and universities compete in collegiate wrestling competitions where the rules are slightly different to Freestyle or Greco-Roman wrestling. For example, there is less emphasis on throws and the point-scoring system is slightly different. The highest level of competition is the Olympic Games, which is held every four years. Olympic medals are awarded for a range of weight classes for both Freestyle and Greco-Roman wrestling for men, and Freestyle wrestling for women. The International Federation of Associated Wrestling Styles, or FILA (*Fédération Internationale des Luttes Associées*) oversees wrestling around the world.

Wrestling competitions test both the skills and stamina of the opponents. Here, two women take part in a competition for the US armed forces.

Glossary

arena an area or platform, usually surrounded by seats, in which sports events, contests, concerts or other entertainment take place.

back arching A quick, powerful movement in which a wrestler pushes their hips under a standing competitor, arches their back and throws the opponent to the mat.

back-step a step and hip-twisting action that turns the wrestler so that they are facing away from their opponent.

bout a wrestling competition, consisting of three periods. In Freestyle and Greco-Roman wrestling, each period lasts for a duration of two minutes.

breakdown a move in which the wrestler attempts to break down the opponent's defences in order to pin their shoulders to the mat.

counter a counter-attack, in which a wrestler manages to stop an opponent's attack and launches their own blocking moves and attacking moves.

drill a practice routine repeated over and over until a set of moves is perfected.

escape moving from the bottom position to a neutral position.

feint feigning, or faking, a move.

folk wrestling a general term used to describe the different types of wrestling found in different regions, cultures and countries.

Freestyle a wrestling style used in international competition.

Greco-Roman a style of wrestling practised worldwide in which the use of legs and feet is limited and no holds are allowed below the waist.

neutral position the starting position in which both wrestlers are on their feet. Neither has any control over the other; also called a neutral posture or stance.

Olympic Games a major international event including summer and winter sports, in which thousands of athletes participate in a variety of competitions.

par terre also called the referee's position, this is the starting position of a floor-based bout where one wrestler is on all fours on the mat with their opponent above them.

penetration a step or forward move to break through an opponent's defences.

pin a move in which a wrestler holds, or pins his opponent's shoulder blades to the mat for a set period of time.

pommelling grappling and grabbing of an opponent's hands and arms to break down their defences.

posture how a wrestler holds his or her body. A good posture will provide a stable platform, without the wrestler being unbalanced.

World Championship the annual FILA Freestyle Wrestling Championship competition.